Exaltation

Abi,
Thank you so much
Always, in all ways.

Exaltation

Michael Indemaio

[signature]

(Don't look down:
We can't turn back)

AVP

Acrylic Verbs Press
New York, New York

Acrylic Verbs Press
New York, NY

ISBN: 978-0-9713503-7-3

Library of Congress Control Number: 2009913367

Manufactured in the United States of America

Contents

Preface

Truth is not a temporary thing bound in time or age or opinion. It does not grow from infancy or shrink at confrontation, does not fade evolve or unwind. There can be no one truth for you and another for me, no variations to suit our fashions and moods.

If truth is to have any meaning, then relativity can not be the single objective fact by which all else falls. Knowledge can not tell us we know nothing, and morality should not be the quality by which we ignore all moral inclinations. If reason concludes that reason itself is limited, it does not follow that nothing is known or knowable. The truth exists regardless, and limits are always from within.

A free humanity uses faith and love and art as tools of transcendence, and lives knowing nothing partial or halved. A free humanity is singing, smiling, dancing, weeping, and laughing. We do not linger in the secret nihilism of subjective truth, where at worst nothing exists and at best nothing exists as fully as can be imagined — where nothing is good or bad and every action is as valueless as every object it affects. We do not malign ourselves with meaninglessness and the freedomless individuality of convenience. We have picnics on blankets trains and trampolines, and we take vacations on carousels.

We start with the self because that's what we are, indivisible individuals actual real and alive, and why should we give that up to the ugly unliving escapism that disavows truth? Instead we are daring and simple and deep. We assume the freedom and autonomy of the individual as an obvious and objective truth, and now the world can breathe. Now we are fully alive and now love exists in every possibility and beauty rests at every turn. Now we are individuals and free to be something more and something better. Now we are free to be something unique and something true, and maybe even something with a soul.

Here I mean life at its highest, the clutch of certain humanity, ecstasy and agony, terrestrial angels unchained. I mean the sound of mankind as it echoes through time and the conscious, unconscious, and subconscious conscience as a mark of the divine. You can find these living souls on every rounded corner of Earth, where art is made and love without pretense, with a determined sense of yearning burning madly loud and wild—and the wilderness of man is civilization, (building and breaking and building again, tribe against tribe against family or friend) and as easy as it is to see havoc, chaos, war, still between the smoke are things which are beautiful and more: a nun that feeds the hungry while a beggar prays to God, and a doctor painting sunsets on a childhood of scars. Community like family is built on humanity (not theory)—and not the other way around. See the homeless smile politely, notice mothers share a laugh, or then soldiers saving children from what will come or what has passed. Witness great musicians as they educate themselves, or the artisans of living making friendships just as well; there is shelter, there is daylight, there are poems on the wall. Feel a moment, know forever— nothing partial halved or small.

Charity is proliferated everywhere humanity survives, and love abounds relentlessly wherever people are alive—and each an individual, each one more than gathered parts. There are reason-based values in this world that are more than arbitrary assignments; they are the choices of individuals deriving meaning from truth. Life has meaning, and the soul has value. The dignity of humanity is not up for debate—you either see it or you don't. It is a basic statement of truth; a revelation of reason on which this earth has worth or it does not. The dignity of humanity is the truth on which every nation must depend and by which all love affairs begin and end. It is the battle cry of liberty, and the width of every art. It is the muse of any charity, and the engine behind peace. It is the reason for compassion and care. Incidentally, it is only in a world of objective truth that it remains beyond dispute. Here it supports equality amongst people of difference, the individuals alive, and the creation of everything of value, from symphonies to universities to the phenomena of carousels.

Carousels, with smiling children spinning much too slow for a thrill, the static grin of horses speared by golden rods, and parents who beam with mock enthusiasm but only the faintest memory of what it truly means to imagine. The carousel is usually built with an uninspired art that is perhaps more honestly called craft. In its finest detail is a creativity that is one part skill and one part chance, but devoid of any expression or semblance of the sublime.

In an empty carousel there is no trace of anything but the carousel and emptiness, and no significance that speaks for itself. It is material and craft assembled as a moving monument to pointlessness. The thing itself makes no sense, not without the children, because in them is the place the carousel only signifies. In them is found the meaning which the thing itself is lacking. Add children to the carousel and you have suddenly an inexplicable beauty —a great mystery to celebrate and enjoy.

I myself remember very much hoping to not be stuck with merely a horse. I wanted to ride a lion, or at the very least a frog. (It would be a magic frog, and that would be the point). The absurdity of the carousel ends when the impossible is actualized in the smile of a child. Not that magic frogs are suddenly real, but that the children in their imagining are more real than anything in the ruthless truthless unworlds of their parents.

At certain carousels, if you arrive for the last ride of the evening, you will see lovers as they ride it side by side. They too have created a world all their own, and in many ways this is a book about those lovers and the world in which they dwell—but here the language fails. This is a book that takes for granted that their world is the real world actualized. It is the only world, where the truth exists regardless of if you accept it. All other worlds are something a little worse than imaginary, and are inhabited by a people who are something a little worse than dead. We can wonder if their love is real, but the simpler truth is that it is occurring. It is happening before our eyes and also somewhere we can't see. What do we mean, is it real? It is, and that's enough. The ceaseless verb of their love becomes the boundless noun of their love, and not only is it a discernable reality, but for the lovers at the carousel it may be the only reality they can imagine.

This is a book that deals with truth and embraces humanity, and I am a person who believes that good things exist, and are therefore attainable. There are literally countless ways to transcend the merely obvious and arrive at the miraculously true, and this is a book that simply believes poetry may be one of them, carousels another.

Shoot Me in the Face I'm in Love

The still photos of your beauty
Are with me everyday—
The smallest units of memory,
The kind of truths I can't replace.

I see you yawning on a bus
And smiling at a friend.
I see you smoking at the park,
Your feet resting on a bench.

And in the tiniest detail
Of your voice and your style
You remind me of a girl who I dreamt as a child.

Something in the way you seem to care,
Your walk, your hands, your hair…
The songs you love, the thoughts you share,
Your optimistic eyes and disinterested air.

I wish I could stop thinking about
Talking about thinking about—
I wish I could stop talking to your eyes.
My severity is cutting me to size.

I see it in my frantic
Every moment to be near you
Awkward fake attempt be easy
Eyes adoring how they fear you, and

I know I've dreamt your motions
(Dreamt your voice, your face, your scars),

I know I've dreamt a girl like you
Being closer than you are;

In my hopes I fear I've dreamt you
In my hopes is what I fear:
The heart rate of your presence,
The helplessness appears,
And in every waking moment
Each digression of my mind,
A dream I had is walking
Talking everything is fine.

And I can't stop thinking of,
Dreaming of, speaking of,
I can't stop talking to your eyes—

So I tell myself it's normal
And I tell myself you're right,
But I can't stop thinking that
        I wouldn't mind
If I let you wreck my life.

I see you standing in the shade
A potted flower in your hands,
And you look at me both lovingly
And as if we've never met before.

Alone

I often say I want to be alone
And don't know what I mean.
It has something to do with forests
And something to do with trees,
But it also has to do with the freedom,
Of birds and their wings.
And as much as it's about lightning bolts
Striking whatever they please,
It's more about the rain,
Emptying streets
And washing them clean.

But Really To Say Hello

If you were attacked
By a band of marauders,
I would try fighting
To save your life.

If you were left stranded
On a small deserted island,
I would go sailing
To say goodbye.

And if you were in love
(oh fear of all fears!)
With somebody else...
I would write letters
To say it's alright.

Reason & Meaning

At the witching time, the darkest hour,
Her eyes are wide and pale,
Her frailest hopes, her widest fears
Screaming through her tears.

I have come to know her meanings
I have seen her broken down,
I know how dreams can dissipate
And I know how days can drown.
When a pillow serves as tombstone
For a grave made snug and warm—
It's not your time, it's not your place;
Everything is wrong.

The highest loves are sadly matched
By the pains that run too deep;
I want to be what keeps her up at night,
But not the reason she can't sleep.

Picture of a Heart

She understands the world
Through its tiniest details
Finding the truth
Through its smallest examples…
And she loves to watch the wind make motion.

Her timeless youth first spoke to me
At its particular age
With the sincerity and aplomb of autumn,
The simple subtle teaching of a phase,
And I found that her silence could move me.

All of this occurred to me
As a single leaf fell
To a thousand ancient footsteps:

How simplicity is made of pieces
Bits of honesty and truth,
And how goodness is a thing at peace
With itself. Whole and actual:
All in its place; all in its part.

I watched the trees stand tall
The subtle breeze swaying branches
And the leaf that fell, as if it wanted
Nothing but to be… just what it was:
The quiet twirling, song of life
Unfettered
I thought, if she were there
We would sit, and say nothing
And I would know I loved her,
Because I would know she saw it too.

Sola Gratia

I found morality while pursuing truth
And truth I found in search of good.
It's a fortunate fact of the nature of Is
That every pure virtue speaks the same yes...

Imagination dripping, eyes just melt
Post-nasal drop, thoughts just felt
Everything happens, the miracle this
Tears of the angels sitting in bliss
Speaking reactions
Withering matters
Momentary fingers that clasp
To revelation that shatters.
The answer to then her interminable why
Came clear through the melting of this magical I
The every expression that I always had meant
The words never spoke and the mail never sent
Because good becomes true because
Yes has no time,
Because always meant is
Because right is divine,
Because good because love
Because some is won't was,
And in matters of why
Because truth is enough.

Lonely Hearts Club

She was there quiet and alone
Sergeant Pepper playing loud
And somewhere I knew was raining.
All around me people talking, groping,
Like being covered with ants
      My flailing ambivalence
Weary and sore trapped in existence
Inescapable homelessness and booze
Mind racing with aching thoughts
Laughter and applause
And then, as the song ended:

I'd love to take you home with me,
But it's much too loud in here.

Detached

We have grown so distant
That now I spend our Fridays
Just watching, detached and confused.
She asks me if I'm okay
But I only see her dancing
To a song I can't hear.
Her lips are moving and I think
She may be asking me again
As she falls on the table and crawls
Like when guillotines turn into kittens
And she hands me her skirt
For safekeeping, as I sip
From the world's smallest straw thinking
"Look, she's sleeping with the band again."

Why are the Beautiful Always Sobbing?

Cause and effect are still indiscernible;
Nonsense talk of how it quite isn't.
The truth is somewhere in the capitalism
Of drug trafficking and
The angry hearts of emotionally abandoned children
Grown—
He said she said he said what he didn't
But the truth is her love was obscured in persistence.
The truth is the years proved the greatest of distance,
And so she cried.

I hung up the phone and swallowed my drink
Knowing her tears didn't make her beautiful
But proved it, like sunshine in June.

The truth is her love is a kind of insistence;
I wanted to cry
But didn't think it would make any difference.

Blue Jay

Then a happy blue jay
Bouncing around the trees,
Jaunting through the drizzling sorrow
And flaunting his wings.

He pointed his beak
Straight at my thoughts
And said
"I could have flown away."

If it's not Good God Truth or Love,
Then I don't want it.

This is where it happened:
        Today.

These private streets of my own design
Saturated and fading
        Away.

Two people searching for love
Never find each other.
One is always in the other's heart
And so they are never together.

Imagine the Godhead descending upon you
—This is what ascension is like.

There was a blue jay preaching
The immediacy of life
As the first rains began to fall,

And I will always choose love
When choosing it is right,
And I would march right through hell
Just to keep it alive.

But please, these questions of yesterday,
These lies of time and inversion—
No more.
Do you want to know what I'm waiting for?

Imagine truth descending;
Imagine hope stored up in clouds.

Christmas Prayer

In the name of the Father
In the name of the just
In the name of forgiveness
In the spirit of love…
In the name of redemption
With immovable faith
For the gift of salvation
Full of mercy and grace,
      I succumb to the world
     And I kneel on my shame
And I open my heart, and release all its pain.

I approach the world humbly
And I suffer my self
And I offer it purely:
All my love, all my wealth,
So to celebrate simply
What I needed the most—
The miracle birth,
Of the existence of hope.

Physical Education

I was never the most athletic child,
Undersized, insecure,
Longing for a book.
Still my highest grade
Came from playing football.

The lesson was the value
Of getting back up.

There

There, in the gutter,
in the rain.
In the stomach,
in the tears.
There, head hung,
strengthless,
faithless:
The World.

Sit with her. Say nothing.
If she asks,
tell her you love her.

The Fall of Allen Ginsberg

I think of doing the math on Wall Street,
Burning chasms of ulcers and tears
Piss-stained dreams of unfurnished rooms
      Windows and doors,
Shut them out, shut them up,
Eruptions and guns, tap-dancing bugs,
Yes, forever is long enough, and wide enough;
You'll find the depths you're looking for,
And now nobody pays rent to Solomon.
Nobody even visits.

I know, it was the fall of Allen Ginsberg,
And we all have that deathly flat autumn despair
Sometimes so ugly, we, human fecal sex fools
Chasing to not get caught when suddenly the truth.
Oh awful, oh hopeless, oh filthy gutter of man.
Please, Creation… take me home.

Millions of miles away, the despair like desert
The sand gets everywhere, homesick,
And to know God never sanctions destruction,
To know fear comes dishonest and cold, and locks
      Windows and doors,
And knowledge was a journey, but now all is old,
Death everywhere, despair like silent poetry,
So far from home.

"Anyone who sees and paints a sky green
and fields blue ought to be sterilized."
—Adolf Hitler, murderer of millions.

See how courses are set, actors direct

The scenes are just that and the time
Ties to death, bound and gagged,
Knotted, locked and unspoken, it wasn't enough
Every heart broken, you have to go mad:
Tomorrow a sunrise —Creation come hear me—
I don't think it's worth it, the travel.

But suddenly, eventually, as sure as we're simple
Emerging perceptually comes tradition inherited.
The predisposition, the nauseous sad dark,
Just process of what we once surely knew,
While louder and louder the moonlight glows
Until finally you hear it all:

The voice behind wind, under leaves, from the now of
Musty pages and busted windows,
Budding flowers shaped like candle flames and
Dim-lit dusky enlightenment fingers cool and jazz
Innocent and pure despite it all
Cut right through, straight and new
Though ancient, though honest,
   Maybe backwards is the only way—
An actual transcendent daisy laughing
Dancing, calling you a fool.

And so I live, and in finite dreams I rest,
   and forever doesn't seem so much.

Tick Said to Tock with a Flick of His Hand

Tomorrow comes with greater speed
As every year rolls by
Time submits and dissipates
To something more derived.
        The hand that sweeps
        The weeping joy
        The buoyant hope
        Of fate alive.

I see mothers nurture children
Just as nature mothers dreams
And the ends we mean to calibrate
Rest on beauties in-between.
        I believe in common magic
        (The miraculous mundane),
        I believe in time transcended;
        No two moments are the same.

I believe in every season
Every leaf that blooms will fall,
And in any single flower
Rests the secret of us all.

(Time is just the way we know
That beauty has no walls).

Break a Heart Open and Count Up the Rings

Ageless child, picker of weeds
Always your love
Comforts and dawns.
In your winters I've trembled
Forgetful and old
  But recall I brought you flowers,
  Unafraid of how we'd grow.

Count As You Pour
But don't mix abstract beauty with abject thought, or,
He Tries for Her to Turn a Vision to a Feeling

Fearing ourselves we find evil's embrace
Drink on our breath, pain on our face
Give up the climb to not feel the fall
Time in our chests, shaming our grace.
Give up on time to not feel so small
Timeless regrets, make-believe walls,
Solitude's safety in a church or a mall—

A corner table yellow light
Another drink a book to write
The falling leaves of local parks
The daily walk through street-light dark,
A favorite chair a hooded head
Curl up calm asleep not dead
A cup of tea, a rhythmic tune
A silent sulk, a silent moon,
And wrapped up warm decay unwind
A banged-up heart, a poisoned mind,
Still unafraid, to look and find
Something simple, something kind—

But fearing ourselves we murder our spirit,
And if you scream out alone,
I promise I'll hear it.

The brief history of the misguided children who choked on their supposed freedoms, or, There's nothing left for you to see, there's no one left for me but me

Destruction brought insipid cheer
   And bang they turned their pain back in.
Destruction came and hid their fear
   And bang they banged their shame to sin.

Destruction came and pain and pain,
    And sweep the streets with tired feet
      That bang and clang the way they came,
     It's hot down here a drink of rain,
     A flame aflame a name a game,
     A way to sell yourself yourself.

A rage an age engaged and caged,
A way to shell yourself enraged,
And no I won't I know I don't,
Your hope is roped in lies to cope—

And bang went the boogie to the boogie man fright—
It's just not the kind of thing, that can happen every night.

Miles of Spit

I see 3,000 miles of liars and spit.
The progression of evil can choke on my wit…

This reality is impossible to conceive;
I perceive, a crack, in their lies.

Whatever is that never was
Is being misled
By a slight of perception,   misdirection.
The question marksman — quite disheartening
     (He arts breaking)
As stutter sparks are weaning sparklings.

This particular poet is obsessing in the rain
Undressing boom bloom pain
     (Yeah the simple rhyme of the forced sublime)
So where's the line that makes a drop

                              drop me?

Any false sense of control has been thrown
Soaked into a corner.
How the simplicity of everyday
Flings about the fierceness of my breathing.

The wisdom of insignificance furthers the connection
To the infinite forever everywhere truth of One,
And there in emerges the only significance,
And in that there is no profundity
It is elementary, and plain,
     And that too may be

A falling back to the top of the circle
        The task of returning where we've never been.
While the misdirection, I assume,
Cloaks complexity in simple rain-gear.

—The sun reemerges but was never in doubt;
The rain is constant, sometimes plotting its form—
This particular no one loves silent and warm
                    frozen and broken
                    tired and worn.

Every new moment is eternity's song.

Man invents nothing
It is all just discovery
And re-releasing myself
Is my only recovery.

        Release from a lie
        From others, from self,
Convention, direction, and what they want me to be,
Assumption, corruption, and what they claim to believe.
No this isn't Buddhist, it's foolish
It is simple and plain:
The misdirection, fakes perfection—
Allow it to soak in the rain.

Being good, and being yourself
Should be one and the same.

(Because evil is not the absence of good...
 Good is never absent).

Fear of Fire

My fear of fire
Is because I've been burnt,

But over time, I'm beginning to learn,
It was always heated metal,
The reckless careless spread
Of a fiery indifference,
Or the absolute arson of hate.

I am saying I'm sorry
If I have feared you,
The candle,
Trying to light my way through.

Fear of Destiny

I am afraid of destiny
Because I've been taught
To mistrust;

I must unlearn the propaganda
That would have me destined
To be someone else.

Fear of the Outdoors

My doubt, I fear
Has been misplaced within
And displaced without.

Since today is beautiful
I will ignore my windows
And embrace my doors.

Fear of Beauty

How can something so pervasive
Concentrate so precisely?

It distracts me,
And divides me,

And I am powerless
When you're beside me.

Fear of Love

Love, I fear losing
May be the hardest thing.

So hard
It may be impossible.

Fear of Fireflies

I wanted to say something.
I wanted to tell her everything.
I wanted to make her a dream
Built entirely of fireflies,

A bright and sentimental charm
She could wear around her fear
To remember a life glowing,
The peaceful flight of beauty and
The magic silent conversation
Of light and love
Which no darkness can stop.

I wanted to, but I was afraid.
Afraid I would catch too few,
Or that she would think I was awful,
For valuing her peace, over their freedom.

I wanted to, but was afraid
And so I sat and watched them
In silent conversation.

Fear of Success

I'm afraid of success
Because I'm afraid of
Emptiness, the unknown
And of being alone.

Success implies an end,
And ends are sad for the joyous.

I enjoy endeavors
Without a ceiling,
The forever windfall of a feeling.
Satisfaction is suicide.

There is never enough
Of what truly we love.

Fear of Carnivorous Zoo Animals

I am always afraid
That those I love
Will be eaten
By a lion or a tiger, at the zoo.

As such
I try not to love those
Who themselves
Have a love for cages.

Fear of The Almighty

My fear of God
Is not for retribution,
But for inadequacy.

Like I cried when my mother
Brought me to see Santa,
Because he knew what I did
But had already given so much,
And I was undeserving.

It feels too much,
Shocking, unthinkable,
To find Him so approachable.

Fear of Heights

Mostly I am afraid
Of abandonment and loss.

That every open confession
Improving the writer
Hinders the ability of love
To hold and to keep,
I confess, is also a fear.

—Let us climb forever higher
The further we go,
Longer the fall,
Greater the fear,
Tighter we'll cling.

Along the long way
I will tell you everything
Hold to your anything
Tremble and whisper:
Don't look down.
I cannot turn back.

Aiming at Honesty

What if I'm honest?

The thought just occurred to me
As if I had an artistic breakthrough.

Not that I'd consider my normal way
Anything like dishonesty,
But what if I switch from intending art
And approaching with honesty,
And begin now to intend honesty
And see if art arrives?
Is that even possible?

I write this at 28 years old
And yet still in a marble notebook,
Crouched in a corner—
The superstitious fetal comfort
Of an artist
Whose confidence has its own moods.

Sometimes I fear I have nothing to say.

Not that I'm afraid of making bad art,
But that I'm afraid of missing art altogether,
And I feel like if I ever fell silent
I would cease to exist.

The artist doesn't know how else to define himself,
And fearing definition the most
He works tirelessly to keep art
Just barely out of reach.

It's probably a productive fear.

Imagination, the once constant natural endless
Dwelling place of childhood
Also grows into a thing to be exercised,
Honed, refined, and mined.
A commodity I'm obsessed with owning
For the sake of art
And at the expense of damned near everything else.
Maybe even at the expense of honesty.
The stated agenda forces me to admit
That I'm not sure.

I don't want to begin now to write about childhood.
I don't want to misrepresent
What was a largely blessed youth
As a bad time when emotional scars first emerged.
Children scrape their knees
And they know what it's worth.

I also don't want to trap myself
Into glorifying childhood
As if it is a more pure state of being,
And adulthood is a waste of paint.
Purity simply becomes a choice and a challenge
Instead of a fact of time.

Maybe imagination is similar.

Still, I can't escape the feeling
That I've grown into a mostly boring adult.
His head in his books,

There are only so many definitions
The artist can take on.

As such, I hate writing about myself,
But they say to write what you know.

Well what else is there for a paper-thin poet?
All I have to work with
Is God, love,
And the drilling of the drying wells of imagination.
This piece is already too long
To make it about God.

I could always make it a love poem,
But I want to resist that too.
Aiming at honesty had a novelty to it
That I don't want to sacrifice
By following my familiar modes of construction.

I rely heavily on a muse,
And a real muse at that.
Not a metaphor,
And not the disembodied goddess
Of the creative spirit,
But an actual someone—
Physical, human, and intelligent.

Sometimes I know her, and sometimes I don't,
But I can always close my eyes and see her,
I can always hear her voice,
And when I fear my own silence,
I can always let her do the heavy lifting.

(Right now her name is Amy,
But I add that bit
Only because I'm flailing at honesty,
Afraid that this one will get away from me).

It's becoming clear to me
That all I do is write love poems,
Either to God, my muse, or myself.
In their absence
I'm left with only the page,
And rather than be silent,
I'll write a love poem to that too.

I wonder if Amy reads my poetry.
I wonder if she prays to God.

Here imagination and honesty have come at odds,
A quandary for the tired artist.
Still, I have to stay the course,
And I can't fill in the gaps of the muse for the muse.
This is not her poem.

This one is for honesty,
And if it lacks punch
It's because I don't have enough secrets.
Nothing good that would leap off the page
And elicit that subtle gasp
That for the reader expresses surprise
But that to me is like you're saying
"My God, *this* is art!"

I don't want to begin writing to you, the reader,

As if this is your poem
Or I know who you are.
(The former is ineffectual,
And the latter dishonest).

I would however like to break suddenly into fantasy.
Something where the muse rides horses
As I stroll overdressed
Through meadows of sunshine
And warm glistening snow.

Of course, it would have to be metaphor,
And I haven't thought that through.
Maybe I don't have the intellect,
Or maybe I just don't care
As much about art
As I think I do.

—Then again, maybe I was right
With all that talk of imagination.
Could that mean
I was also right about choice and challenge?

I suppose the horses symbolize freedom,
And a connection with nature.
An at both times tame and wild
But still earthly beauty.
Plus, girls love horses,
So we can assume she's fairly content.

My strolling probably implies leisure,
But at the same time

I'm not the one riding
On freedom's back.

What am I doing there anyway?
I hope I was invited.
Obviously the meadow is beautiful,
But only because my muse is also,
And the meadow must fall in place.

It is both sunny and snowing
Because the scene must present
An unattainable perfection.
This underscores the metaphor
And reinforces how we're really only representing
My feelings,
And you the reader can read beauty
Into their child-like naiveté.

Knowing all this may be why
I've arrived overdressed.

I should have specified
If I was in an out of place tuxedo
Or perhaps an all white suit
(Symbolizing purity,
And drumming up an imagistic reference
To more chivalrous times).

—Amy is actually here, physically, right now.
She arrived halfway
Through the last stanza,

But I'm ignoring her
To concentrate on the poem.
Partially because this isn't about her,
And I have to stay diligent,
But also because in real life
She petrifies me.

Maybe that is why I'm overdressed.

I wonder what it's like,
To be as free as a muse,
With all those horses.

I feel trapped in art,
Or at least like it dictates my life
In a way that may be unhealthy.
This won't be the last time
I ignore a muse.

Running from life in order to write about it,
Is that dishonest?
All those pages?

Will a thousand poems make people think
I must live a full life?
Really it should indicate the opposite
(If I was holding her hand
I wouldn't be holding this pen),
But most people don't see that.

Last week I decided to title a poem,
"You're always on the other side of rain."

I haven't written it yet,
And I haven't even decided what the title means.
I just know that's how it goes with muses.

Now that I've mentioned the title,
I may not actually write it.

It seems like the stanzas of this poem
Are getting shorter as I go on.
Maybe I'm getting tired.
Maybe later I'll go back
And break some of the early ones in half.

Maybe I won't
In order to give this one its effect.

(I eventually changed all the stanza lengths
And added more line breaks, and
Then I added this in,
After the poem was complete.
I could have removed the whole section,
But I wanted to show how honesty
Is sometimes mundane).

I'm just trying to maintain a continuity,
Which I think is important in art.
When a stand-up comic references a joke
From earlier in the set
They tend to get a big laugh.
In the same way,
Now would be a good time
For me to mention my notebook,

Because that was from far enough back
The reader may have forgotten it.

The talk of fetal comfort
And my lack of confidence
Can now stand in a new light,
Because Amy is here by herself
And I am here with my notebook.

I once had a muse
Who didn't scare me as much.
One night I was talking
With a friend about this muse,
And the friend asked me
"Do you think she's trying to keep you happy,
Or just inspired?"
And I said,
"I don't know that there's a difference."

I'm beginning to learn
That there is a difference,
But that you can't tell a muse how to work.

Aiming at honesty,
Continuity, and art,
(In that order)
I'll attempt to end this poem,
By talking about the difference:

Happiness is where we both ride horses,
And if I ever write that poem,
Where both of us are free,

I'll use my title…
I'll switch the warm glistening snow
To warm shimmering rain,
And that will be the only thing that separates us—
Her ability to stand in a place
(The other side of rain)
That I can only imagine,
And say in words.

Because beauty as seen in another
Is a dimension all its own,
Transcending our boredom and walls.
To get it from ourselves,
We have to put it somewhere else…
Therefore, art.
I am inspired by the beauty I lack.

Good art is honest
Because art is by nature a little dishonest.
Beauty in a bottle.
Freedom in a cage.

Inspiration only points me
To the places I can't say,
While happiness is smiling in the rain.

Me, when I'm happy,
I will find freedom by shedding my fears.
I will put my notebook away.
I will shut up and listen.

I will know that the truth is walking.

A Single Light

In the cold white depths of winter
In the silence of night,
There was a single light left on
Guiding me home.
Everything seemed swept
With its warm and soothing glow,
And it was beautiful
Because I know—
I know why the light was left on.

Direction

In New York City
Uptown and Downtown
Aren't just places,
They're directions.
If you're going from 125th street
To 116th street,
Downtown is where you're heading.

This is what I mean
When I talk about Heaven.

A Prayer For New Love

Let this feeling remain, let her
Always shine this newly lit
Joy of what is found.
Let her keep with faith, (she has
Such faith), let her keep always
Her dutiful heart, not burdened,
Not hardened, not weighted with hate,
And if fate, or something lower,
If it should need a wage, please
Withdraw it from me.
Let my love remain free.

As even You, glorious strength
In this very humanity, You bore
All sin and iniquity, the pain of a world,
Giving entirely, even to death
You suffered our burden,
And shouldered our hurt,
Not lightly, not grandly
Not in obedience or madly,
But in this very humanity,
With something more;
Every thorn of this world, You wore.

So let the wage be paid, and not by vows
But by the hearts from behind them.
Not by mere people, or words—
But by love—by that which can bind them.

Steeple

The church steeple rises to tap the sky
Where I knew the truth of truth in an instant,
Watching the sun hold the old steeple
Playing softly grandly its heart-swelling song
Not ancient woodwinds and strings, not
Organs and incense or ornamental robes
But an actual modern song of heart, and real,
A rock and roll ditty like I could never write
But which I knew came from me, only me,
And also from not me, from the
Deepest of inside and the highest of above
Coming from just beyond that impossibly high
Church steeple tapping the sky shining its song
Saying go, move, reach, rise, soar—
And then my heart alive, fearless, in love
Everywhere at once, and now set alight,
Tapping to the melody of miraculous sky.

What Love Knows

I watch the children, see they love without reason
And think how sad it is
That they will have to unlearn this.

Love is irrational, in its nature
And so we learn to outthink what we feel,
Because the truth is the truth is
Something too large to be held,
And we all need to hold on to something.

I say that I am overwhelmed by the beauty of the world
And she says that she is sick with the feelings in her heart,
But what love knows,
Is that we've both just said the same thing.

Roast and Remain;
The city that burnt me to the ground

Now is the season of roast and remain;
The city that burnt me to the ground.

Danger Ms. Robinson: the matchsticks of Hell.
Evil becomes
An unbecoming undone,
And I am the waters,
And here comes the sun.
The tides of tomorrow, the drying of sin;
The sawdust of Babylon
Washed away from within.

They've been gathering darkly, sinister grins—
The acidic corrosion of nothing begins.
So away with your sorrow,
Away with your fear,
As the nearer they draw,
The more clear they appear.
Revolution is cycling.
Restitution is near.

Because the truth is the fires
Engulf and surround,
And I've climbed up their towers
And I've swallowed the ground.
I've heard the sound of their echoes,
Their emptiness screams,
And I've climbed up their hatred
And swallowed our dreams.

And now is the season of roast and remain

—I've put my head in the clouds to return as the rain—

And pain knows no limit
Through the limits of fate
And pain knows no wisdom
That is worth its own wait.
>   There is freedom in waiting
>   There is laughter in choice
>   And the deafening nothing
>   Will be shattered by voice.

>   So away with your sorrow
>   And give voice to your heart;
>   In the ashes of pain
>   Is where faith gets its start.

Redemption Doesn't Know Me;
She has subtle poignant eyes

These first few lines are to establish my pain.
Gravel on the shoes of tired knees.

The sorrowful sparrows whistle an ominous tune
As an alley cat playfully slaughters a mouse,
And I stumble my way
To a workweek of welcome routine.
Everyone I love is broken.

Without a home, the world becomes wider
Violent and grey, and
Death hangs as moistly
As the mundane evil we have to swallow
In polite conversation, mass-transit, and rain.
Meanwhile, time cuts through life
Like a machete through shrubs:
Reckless and precise.

As the weight of the selfish and the way of destruction
Just begin to crumple me, exhausted
I see you and smile,
As you interrupt the rain
As if to say, "Beauty can accomplish anything
And has already defeated death."

And although I've only just met you,
You have meant to me the world.
You have reminded me
That eternity was built for moments.

Love Poem

Everything I've ever said
Might be a lie

Except for this:

I think I love you
And I don't know why.

Walking By

I saw you walking by
But pretended I didn't.

I want you to know:

I can't bear to see
What I can't stand to let go.

6 Conversations with the Beloved

1. Will you marry me?
   No.
   Will you go to a movie with me?
   Maybe. Are you going to ask me to marry you again?
   Not at the movie, no.

2. Do you like fish?
   Yes, why?
   I was going to buy you a fish tank.
   Oh, I meant I like them dead, as food.
   Well, do you like me?
   Yes… why?

3. Why do you love me?
   Who says I love you?
   It's the only explanation.
   I suppose it is.
   So why do you love me?
   As soon as I figure it out I'll stop.

4. Has anyone ever said you're beautiful?
   You did, about an hour ago.
   Good, just making sure you remember.

5. Right now, I'd believe anything you say.
   Okay, you're a radish.
   Is that a good thing?
   They're my second favorite vegetable.
   What's your first?
   Probably Johnny Depp.

6. Will you marry me?

No.

Would you marry Johnny Depp?

No.

Why not?

Because he's not you.

That doesn't make any sense.

As soon as I figure it out I'll tell you.

What am I to do until then?

You can buy me that fish tank.

Rhythm

There's something in rhythm,
Something in motion.
      We're not meant to sit still.

The way a bass-line backbones a song
Always playing onward,
Singing: motion, forward, go.

In our lives we're never happy
With the last great success,
Never safe in a day like the last.

We must build forever higher,
We must grow from now to now
Only looking to the past, for clues on where to go.

I'm convinced it doesn't matter
How a life chooses to proceed,
It's the rhythm that informs it
      Which is all we ever need.

Where Does Love Come From?

Thoughts are compiled one on the other
Systems and theories,
The intricate ways that we know,
Are formed through the ages
Filling nations and souls.
I'm long past the issues
        Of meaning and purpose
What is moral or noble,
What is honest or worthy.
Love is the value, by which all else is measured,
The reason inherent in all great endeavors.

And so in my quest for a more perfect question
I can't help but to think what we seek is its source.

Know the source of all love,
And you'll know why you're here.
Know what love is most like,
And you'll know why you feel.

There's no meaning in anything, unless it is love,
And humanity gets nowhere without it.
Know where love comes from,
And we'll know where to go.

Composed and Decomposing

I have still a pile of poems,
Scattered ink stains of inconsequence,
Unused and decomposing,
And I start to feel like nothing lives
Until it's useful and acknowledged.

Somewhere in this country
I have family, lost
Touch; lost feeling.
I loved them once
As a child, surely
Which is better, more sure,
And also my action-figures
Crated up in boxes of time gone by.

They too were once alive, infused
With my infatuous imagining
Like the love I hold for you,
Desperate thoughtless dreaming, Pinocchio love
My last great pretend, slowly
Bit by bit undoing itself
Back to the nothing from which I called it.

I always wake a little sore and unsure
What to do with the dreams that never were.
With the past at rest in boxes
The blank page becomes today. A present;

And if all that was is lost,
Then all that remains must be found.

Sparky in a Tin Can

Sparky is in a tin can,
Cremated into a shelf-piece,
And it seems an ignoble end
For a dog that had such fight.

I always felt regret
For naming her that,
A clichéd title
For a dog that never tamed.

I named my next dog Sonnet
And she romps playful and innocent
Oblivious to her predecessor
Who once patrolled these quiet halls,
The proud warrior in a tin can.

I look at it sometimes,
With her picture taped to the side.
A tiny monument to her liveliness;
The remains of her significance.

I trudge through these slow human years,
As if leashed to my memories
And my strictly human concern for legacy,
Petrified I'm doing it all wrong.

When I'm gone, and another occupies my purposes,
I hope at the least one love will linger
Just because I was.

Heartbeat like a Head Wound

Late night thoughts of you, subdued
Until a message comes across the screen,
My heartbeat like a head wound,

And you, something nonchalant
Brilliantly vague that could mean
You love me

Or that you can't sleep, you're awake
Thinking of someone else
And what does it matter?

Love is not a game, no,
My heart bounced like a ping-pong ball

You are too much at joy to love at all;
No one in love could smile like you,
And no love could be so light or calm and

I'm jealous of where I don't know you are.
I am angry at my weakness in the face
                              Of your smile

And maybe you just want me to reply
And feel you don't know me.

There is such distance between us
And when our hands first touched

How accidents are never just coincidence,
It was easy then, to notice something grand,

Something chance couldn't explain,
How we met or where we'd land
—You have to try to understand.

Love is a dangerous cure for a headache...
Please, don't play russian roulette with my heartbreak.

When It Hurts Too Much

I'm tired of being this feeling
And I'm tired of feeling this low. Depression is who I am.

I've tried to not admit how bad it is
And what used to be inspiring has rendered me speechless.

I'm tired of struggling for voice
And being embarrassed and inarticulate.

I don't care if I write bad poetry today
And I don't care if I vomit or bleed to death.
                                        I'm sick and I have to get it out.

I don't care if there's no metaphor,
Because nobody pays attention.

The words are the thing in themselves. I was taught that
By the same people who told me to show it, not say it.
They made me feel invisible, and I don't care about them
Anymore.

I'm feeling a little unstable,
Because the sadness is too much and I can't think.
                                        It's choking me.

I don't want to write about love, just loneliness—
Nothing about heartbreak but actual disappointment
                                        And deception.

Not dead flowers but paper-mâché—and they catch fire—
And the smoke... and I choke.

And I mean that too,
About trial by fire and the burden of the cross,
Pain and gain and the deepest strength of the soul

But I mean that I am being strangled and it feels like death.
I mean release, not triumph.

I mean give me the morphine and let me sleep.

Take away this feeling or take away me,
Because I can't see one for the other.

It's just pain. It doesn't *mean* anything.

Notes on Your Friendship

I was honest with you, told you the truth,
Because with your determined capacity
For being yourself

I thought you might think of me differently,
And might think of me less,

But knew you would never think less of me...

It may be I'm incapable
Of being a good lover,
Destined to remain an insignificant other,

　　But with you that never felt like a crime.

Sometimes I feel both surrounded and lonely,
And heartbreak and love both only make me feel worse;

I've kept every gift that you ever bestowed me,
With the hope I'll grow into their worth.

Eyesight to Behold Her

Beauty is most emphatically not
In the eye of some beholder,
As if just a thing imagined,
As if something less than real.

I have seen you stroll Manhattan streets
As if you didn't have a care,
And in the dim and dirty shadows
Of that insomniatic city
You shone brighter than compare.

I have seen this more than felt it;
It was real and I was there.

The beauty I have seen in you,
Is not a matter of opinion.
It's a question of who notices,
And how acute might be their vision.

Tricks on Me

If I walk through Times Square
I will think I see your face
At least twice in the crowd,
    And I know you're in another city.

When you're gone my heart goes crazy

And my imagination takes me
From sadness how it can.

I am sure you'll always love me
No matter how much we're apart

But I'm not sure if it's justified
Or just a delusion of the heart.

Bad Dinosaur Was Born On Dinosaur Island

"Bad Dinosaur was born on Dinosaur Island,"
A child tells his father,

      And they both understand the importance.

The moral is in the subtext
And the joy is in the telling,

And Bad Dinosaur grew up an orphan
Who never had anyone to talk to.

An Easy Way to Die

At first a light desire,
Introduced as whimsy and abandon
Which began to make excuses
As a habit unrestrained,

But when it claimed itself essential
To accomplish who I am,
It had grown to something violent,
And Addiction was its name.

And now I never wrote, and never lived…
Or at least not how my vices did.

No Peace for Halfway Dreams

I hereby declare war
      On the dull and uninspired,

And on every aching moment
Spent at home in moderation

        —There will be no peace for halfway dreams.

The world can break my heart again
In any way it can;
Take away my comfort,
Or take away my air.
      It can take me to the brink of death, so long
           As I'm taken to a brink,
              I don't care.

    Let no chance be bound by circumstance,
    Let no stone remain unpainted,

  Anything realistic is just a goal already tainted.

I will love at the rate that hate creates weapons
(I will have freedom or safety—not both),
I will make my mistakes but then never regret them,
There is no way to beauty but growth.

When I First Met Her

When I first met her she wore a summer skirt
With those wintry boots
        Naked Eskimo in linen, nothing matched,
And I asked her why so many migrate from her home state.

She said they were trying to escape, and I thought
She's stupid, like all the rest,
Expert witness to the guilt of her village, but then
In the same instant I thought it clever,
Them escaping freedom and expanse for urban trappings.
                Baffling minx…

She had confused me about the value of a phrase
And on that my soul's livelihood depends,
              Knowing the worth of words.
Destructive woman,
She walked with such speed and no explanation
Near enough that I could sense her warmth
  Like the warmth that comes from deep inside things—
Gutted animals and molten lava—
      The warmth of a boundary crossed.

Fiery uninvited Eskimo,
When I first met her she confused me,
But when she left
          The world felt boring and cold.

70

America I Love You

America I love you, you impossible beast
You invisible dream always just out of reach.

I often can't see you but hear you
As a choir of voices singing the mad rumbling
                                        Yes of creation.
My God we're alive aren't we?
Walking breathing touching feeling
Vomit-stained incidents of love and loss,
Items of depression and ecstasy—
Life is not what we're wading through life is what we are;
I see communities of longing as terrestrial stars
Clusters of light scattered haphazard and bright
On a blanket of fields all dark and all possible
The patchwork of a nation and the fabric of a dream.

From the last window seat of a miniature 757
I am struck by the space between towns
The emptiness like labored breathing,
Like the meaning when reading between the lines.

Each garden of light sprouts up at unexpected turns
Clinging to rivers and roadways
As a reminder of dependency, and necessity,
And I can hear the choirs singing
                                See their starlight dance
And it's as if they've come together for the company
Huddled around each other's lights for warmth—
The thick and earthy warmth of humanity,
        The always immaterial light of manmade hope.

It is nothing but people sitting around campfires

And lounging on old wooden porches,
This dream we keep grasping at,
This America we've stitched together with discarded pieces,
Just as sure as 90 story apartment complexes
It is but a coming together, a comforting place,
An embrace in the wild,
                              In the limitless space,
In a world where alone we can't imagine its scope,

Where we still fear at any moment
The oceans might swallow us whole.

I'm Sick of Your Emails
When No One Else Will Listen

You write me with no punctuation,
    Which is your way,
To say something I've never understood.

Your timeline is skewed
Like when we would argue, and

The fog rolls in off the ocean,
And I realize I don't owe you anything.

I respond to say
Your letter arrived several years late

And no one here can translate
That archaic language
                  Anymore.

Poet

A poet is a person
Who toils with words
Until they match a feeling.

A good poet, is a person
Who doesn't care
Where that feeling came from.

Solitary Music

I spent a Wednesday in the city
Alone in crowds of hip and glam,
Playing parasite to the joy and energy
Of young and emerging bands.

After three and countless drinks
I felt dizzy and anonymous,
Like I couldn't find the ground.

The jazz guitarist who drove my taxi
Said he was very glad to meet me,
And then, stopped at a red light,
He played the national anthem,
On a harmonica, saying

"I love music…
It cost me my life to do this."

Dust Me Off

Dust me off I've had enough
I know you're beaten down by love
Don't look for God in skies above
A faith unclear, a place to run,
A constant fear of things now done
With bold abuse and cold untruth
Too old for death, too young for youth
Hate is none and love is one
It's all the same: your pain, your shame,
The blame that plays its hurtful game
Can never dry forever's rain
You've always known your makers name.
He's everywhere, in every thing
The tears we cry, the songs we sing,
The love we build, the pain it brings,
A sparrow's heart, a flower's wings,
In all the things that Go(o)d can bring—
While evil crowns itself a king.

So please let's stand, hand in hand
One by one we'll understand
There's only truth, no greater plan:
Man isn't God… but God *is* man.

—With the greatest stroke of the greatest brush
God's heart broke, and all this was.

So dust me off, I've had enough…
Because I was made, to the tune of love.

Atrophy and Joy

As a child we tend to believe
What the other children think
To be true.

As a result, our peers can redefine us,

And as an adult,
      I once managed to do this to myself.

I began to feel like a failure
Or worse, like someone quite average,
And eventually
This belief became true;
I had shrunk into my own low expectations.

      But by chance or by fate
          (And I prefer to think fate)
   I could never quite stay in one place—

And a body in motion continues in motion…
And an object of faith finds its grace.

      I'm not really sure how I found you my love
      But I'm sure it was you that found me—

I mean it was you who uncovered my truth,

And I remember the day you introduced me this way:
You said, "this is my love, he is also an artist,"

And I thought nothing could sound more like fact.

Of course I knew I was an artist,
Just not that it was secondary,
As in, "he is her love and an artist as well."

An artist, a failure, and average,
An ape with a spirit and mind.
But above all of this, in that moment,
I became what I wanted to be.

You called me your love
And that became who I was,
Because I knew we both thought it was true.

In that all my doubt was supplanted by joy
And all goals became within reach,

Because real love makes everything
Seem tiny and possible,

And you will be humbled to know who you are.

Replaying Your Words

I can't shake you from my mind
Although only half of me is trying…
The other half replays your words
Again and again in my head,
More like a record than a riddle.

Last night for the first time
I didn't break eye-contact
With the pretty faces on the
Opposite direction trains,
Because I guess I had nothing to hide.

My eyes keep begging for help
Because this longing is burning
And I know LA is laughing at your jokes,
While all of New York just looks at me mistrustingly.

I think my loneliness is growing with my popularity.

I can't hear the phone or television
Or the noise of my dreams,
And I lay awake for hours with the radio off
Counting your sheepish expressions.

I take them with me
Exhausted through the day
        And all I can hear is your voice.

You say that you love me, and you talk about trust,
But you also keep asking,

"Will you still be you, when I get back to us?"

Questions of Faith

The child wants to know
If Jesus was without sin
            Why he didn't cast the first stone,

And I say that He came to forgive, this time.
                Judgment comes later.

The kid's sister says if He was divine
Then it kind of diminished His sacrifice
    And I say He was also fully human
    The pain was real and was nothing
Compared to the pain of divinity
Feeling detached from divinity
            The pain He expressed in that question
                About forsaking,

And their father
    He wants to know what Jesus does
    With the money from the baskets and such
                Because he's mad at the church.

I just talk about the root of all evil
And how the meek shall inherit the earth,

    And let them ask me these things
    As if they were asking a priest,
    Because it's our duty to answer for our faith.

But if you asked God
        Too many questions
He might answer you as if you were Job,

Like when you'd criticize your father,
Or if you called your dean a liar:

He'd remind you who you're talking to
And that He doesn't have to explain Himself to you.

He'd ask you what exactly you've accomplished
That lets you question Him,
                                        And then

He'd leave you in your ignorance
To contemplate your arrogance.

The Love of Money

The love of money is the root of all evil
Where money is wealth not found in God
And love is just lust in a top hat.

(Because lust is to greed
As love is to charity,

And God is to beauty
As lies are to flattery).

She Grew Homesick and Uncertain

You said the city smells of hotdogs and dog crap
And I was certain you were leaving.

Now I pick up where you left me,
As if asleep but not yet dreaming,
And I walk these empty highways
Littered without meaning.

I just can't justify my sadness,
For your happiness without me
Is still happy nonetheless,

And it's better to have been loved and left
Than to watch love dying where it stands.

It's Been Raining Since I Met You

Paul asked if I was sad it's all over
And I'm not sure why but I said no.

I don't want you to make me sad or admit that you have.
If they ask if I'm heartbroken I'll say "no
         She wouldn't do that,"
And anyway where do they get off
Rubbernecking vultures texting their votes to my pain.
Nothing is like it was and I've never felt the same.
I hate to admit how much I hate when things change.

I'm not used to this summer, it doesn't feel like it's real.
Too far gone in this life I've found myself trying to go back,
Following breadcrumbs and tugging at lifelines,
Because I don't feel like myself,
         Don't recognize my laughter,
And I hate you for making me feel so young and alive.

I don't want to be inspired in the summer
         And I don't want the summer at all.
I don't want you picking flowers
And dancing to what must be a tune in your head.
                                    You're always dancing,
And even when you're not
There's a rhythm and grace about you that I can't imagine,
                         Offbeat as I am,

And I don't want to take the flower
From your delicate hands
                         And place it in your hair.
I don't want to be writing this

And I won't write anymore when we're gone.

I don't know who I write to anymore, is it for you or for me,
And if it's for us (there is no us),
        Why does the world need to read it?

I'm always writing letters to the world
And I don't want them looking at me.
—I just write so I know where I am.

These are ancient syllables,
And Lord knows you can make me feel old.

I've been watching the breeze through the trees
For more years than I know,
And the problem is that one wind is unlike every other.
No matter what the pattern, there is no consistency.
        Day to day, season to song,
Until I can't stand to see you shiver in the rain
Or the clocks that spin while I wait for your call.
I am anxious for autumn;
I hope it feels like it used to
With nothing new and everything folding and sleeping,
And there will be no flowers and no footprints
And everything will be comfortable and done,
And myself as a child getting ready to die.

Dearest world… take my letters to heart.

Heed please my warnings on the madness of love,
Poets falling mindless on the thick and jealous grass,
        Lapping up sunshine with a gluttonous rage.

There are pigeons on the pavement,
                              Homeless as the day is new,
Families strolling carelessly,
And the thick humid laughter
Of the summer's haughty breeze —please—
         Never let these letters go unnoticed
         Through the seasons of debris.

The kings of the earth have gathered together
         At the bookstore
And their violence is for anyone certain and alive.
I have mastered a new trick,
Where I stand perfectly still as I run.

The poets grab their words and throw them in sacks,
Slowly making their way to the asylum,

And I've never felt less confused than in this moment,
Standing here, motionless,
Watching the world grow smaller and smaller
As the sunlight melts my mind like so many ice cubes.

The poets sit in tunnels reading books on local trains,
And as the night falls,
I whisper goodbye,

And the world has gone to sleep.

Understanding

Mothers who know how to father
And fathers who know how to mother

Have children who know how to love.

Certain Truths

Not so much streets as giant concrete hills,
A walk around North Beach is a hike
From which at certain heights you can see simple truths

Like why we climb.

The way back down is easy
A reckless stumble
Like all triumphs

And maybe if I spill my coffee
We'll laugh

Because it's always worth it for the view.

Time Seals all Tombs

Some people are young in such an impermanent way
And you can see how intense they watch each other
With a kind of purpose for aimlessness
And a passion for living
                    If not yet life.

Soon you'll cut your hair and remove
The stripes from your shirt.

You will let the holes in your ears and your nose
Conform to society, like your minds,
                            As they close.

You will learn to mistrust, not just hatred,
But love,
        And you will fear whatever seems pleasant or fun.

It's okay, it's normal. Just remember who you were,

Because if you don't see how people can change by accident,
You'll never learn how you can do it on purpose.

A Thousand Meals without You

Dinner is the worst
When everyone can see where you're not sitting.

The waiter asks if I'm waiting for someone
And then removing the extra silverware, says
"Let me just take away the ghost."

                                    But you're never really gone.

As Two become One, Three become Two

"She made me a mix" he tells me, violent
Like stomping on someone's foot
Smug and proud

And I say, "she made me one too,"
                   But you didn't.

It was really just a copy of his.

New Beginnings and Old Habits

In a new city I'm tired from walking
When I enter the quietest café I can find
Lining up for coffee and lunch.
Behind the counter her eyes are as sad as downtown,
But it could just be the afternoon crowds.

She's dressed for work as if to say
She doesn't care to meet me,
But she smiles and says she'll bring me my food—

Deep bright eyes framed
By the loose strands of her sunset hair
Beautiful and American (west coast but not western),
She is prettier than her city but in the very same way.

I keep waiting for the restroom
But every time I look up
Someone else beats me to it
And now on my third coffee
                    (Each more awkward than the last)
And I should say something but can't
And someone else keeps beating me to it
And her glances are making me nervous
And if I didn't have to go now I'd go—
Finally
        I hop up and walk casually to the restroom,
And having noticed others struggle
I give the door a firm tug
                    Not wanting to attract
                    Any extra attention

    …And the doorknob falls off in my hand.

I take it with me and place it on the counter.
She smiles, and I say I'm sorry,

I always have trouble with openings.

One Too Many Mirrors

There's one too many mirrors in this hotel room
And I'm wearing a ten year old shirt.
It was my favorite then and I thought
I'd feel young but I look so old
    And everything dies
    Even living creatures
    Like love letters yellowing in a storage box
    And I wonder where you are
    And if you wear your wrinkles as well
    As you once wore this shirt
        And I'm sorry that I never brought you flowers.

I guess everything is growing or it's wilting,
And you know I would have died for you
                    That's easy.

I'm just sorry I never lived for you.

Upon a Lost Violet (the freedom and joy of the water)

I knew a violet who was born of the sun and the soil
And who would always speak to me, on warm afternoons,
Of her love for the rain,
      Which nurtured her
And which filled her with hopes and dreams.

We would sit together for hours then,
      Until sunset,
And I would warn all the onlookers:

No matter how beautiful you find her,
          You must not pick her.

Even if your beloved wants nothing more
Than a bouquet of the finest violets,
Still you must refrain—
This one must remain unharmed, and free to grow.

If they would question me further, I would explain:
She dreams of only rain. The freedom and joy of the water.

She wanted only to be washed clean of the soil
And to be comforted from the burn of the sun.

Earlier this evening I saw her in the river.
That is, the river was her then.

She was hunched over the horizon
Resting her head on her arms, waving.
A wave like an inescapable thought,
The kind of thought that swells so constant and rhythmic
You forget who you are.

I am not a river
But just the rhythm of these waves;
This is not my lifetime
But just a collection of my days.

Repetition builds itself into a false kind of constancy,
But true constancy never ends, and never repeats.

There, floating in the wake of her wave
Were four petals from her past—remnants of a feeling,
The now mere memories of a once bright garden.

I watched them with a faint smile,
Like one who smiles at the sick
With toothy grin
But sad and frowning eyes.

I see she has finally washed away, I said,
I see she has joined the river, and as such become it.
But where does she go?

And I was answered by each petal,
As one at a time,
They sank into forever…

"She goes to the ocean."
"She will be comforted."
"She waves goodbye."
"You must not follow."

Why? Why?! I questioned—why must I not follow?

Until in an instant, I answered myself:

Of course… she dreams of only rain.
The freedom and joy of the water.

I watched, as one at a time,
My tears fell down to where the petals had been.
My small contributions to a distant and unknowable beauty.

As they vanished into the calming waters,
My heart beat in waves of sorrow
            —The inexplicable rhythm of my pain.

I knew then
That I would someday sit in gardens,
Entertaining onlookers

With stories of the greatest violet I'd ever known,
And the supreme lesson she taught me:

How no amount of sorrow, can ever achieve,
The constancy of any love.

Solitude is Something we Share

Where did all the years go, the leaves all dry and windblown?
How I never meant to let you blow away.

I spent what seemed like lifetimes
Searching for your smile
And I knew it in an instant,

But when I looked into your eyes
I saw that beauty found in nature
Is almost always wild.

—You, my heartsick nomad,
I know you must keep moving

As I live alone in crowded cities

Feeling closer for our distance.

Dead Birds on the Sidewalk

Brooklyn has been known to taunt me
With dead birds
             Signposts and warnings

Saying, "Do Not Enter
Past one in the morning

                  Do you really think you'll find her
                  Drinking domestic beer
                  From a plastic cup
                  On Bedord Ave?"

A woman asks if we've met before
And I say I don't think so
And walk away.

My mood is dropping now,
And I know I'll always be alone.

I put my headphones on
Sit at the corner
And crash.

Diamond-Studded Nightmare

Dear diamond-studded nightmare
Choking vision of my failure
It's high time we've had this talk.

I can't see the paths abandoned
Through your nagging echoed spite,
Discarded sentiments of etiquette,
Nights you've stretched around my neck.

I was snatched out of my cradle
A bassinet I never owned,
And was told, yes told, where I would grow:

In a corporate bit of plastic
Cage of steel and tinted glass;
Giant crystal castles,
Haunted mansions taunting sky.
But no one asked me what I wanted.

Diamond-studded nightmare, please
I swear I'd rather die.

Drab numerical cathedrals
Post-war ceilings on my mind,
I won't and can't, I—
They said inalienable rights.
But it's not a bid for happiness, please,
Please do not mistake me.

I have to break for freedom,
For the pursuit, my pursuit, my right.
—I am the sacred hunter, not you!

It's for primal basic urges,
Caves of flesh and bones,
The matted dirt of yearning,
Blades of grass flat under toes, listen—
Whitman speaks to people who don't even know he existed;

In the ether of America,
In the background of their lives, on
Coffee-stained sweatshirts and oxygenated paint
Sprawled across the bricks of their ancestors,
Immigrant songs of right and wrong and
Impotent cries of I belong.
                                This
Is my nation, if not my destination.
        I am tendering my resignation.
Resigned to the fact, that you owe me myself.

Look, I don't want what Whitman had,
I just need what I believe.
        There's still space enough to save us
        And I intend to breathe.

I Know a Snowman

I know a snowman
Who goes north for the summer,
Who has two younger siblings
A sister and brother

Who have the very same names
As the kids up the street
Who themselves have a brother
Who comes home on the sneak

To build a family of snowmen
That the children agree
Returns every winter
If good children believe.

Broken Heart Healed

What does a heart look like once it's been healed?
How does a soul express, what God has revealed?

Well it starts with a rhythm from somewhere within him,
And like anything true it knows no division—
Truth doesn't come in pieces.
It comes with connection that multiplies meaning,
And meaning just means that we've ended a search;
Sometimes to get to our best
We have to go through our worst.

I've seen the tears of an angel on the cuff of my shirt
And felt the stars in my eyes with my ear to the dirt,
And I felt like the pain would always remain,
(Keeping me stuck in metaphorical rain),
But no matter how much it seemed my heart broke enough
Try as I might I just couldn't cure love,

And oh what a meaning, what a thing to believe in,
The more that I see it I can't help but to be it.
I can't help but to hold it but to want it and own it,
And oh how it heals me, how it knows and reveals me—
This is the very first poem that I wrote for you.

I know I do not have to love you but I just can't help but try,
I've held the world in my heart by the skies of your eyes,
And the flowers keep blooming to call winter a lie.

So now is the summer of the pain I once felt
Cycling holy through the stars I was dealt;
Fear and confusion can shine as they melt
And this little light of mine

...Makes a shadow of Hell...

Because Heaven is here and Heaven is now
When we stop asking why,   to find a more beautiful how.

And here is the secret of a heart that won't quit:
Love is the meaning of all that exists.

Midnight at the Blue Lady Lounge

We were in our early twenties
When we began to spend time
At the quietest bars on the quietest nights
Listening to Johnny Cash and indie rock.

It seemed like no one had a job
When really no one had a care

And we were there to laugh and love.

This night my friends sat to my right
While I talked with a middle-aged gang member
Drunk enough to tell me he was

       And they all knew how I felt
       That you can learn from anyone you meet
       And there is light in every darkened soul

But we were just sad young men
       Reckless and naive
With no one to love but our friends,

And the only woman there was the bartender
Mixing drinks for us to name.

When the pudgy thug said I could join his gang
I could tell that he was lonely.

He would bark like a dog
When he was proud, (or just being loud),

And he said that we were brothers
And had to look after one another,

Before stealing all the money off the bar.

I chased him up the street, and screamed,
"Hey, I thought that we were brothers!"
            And he stopped to ask me what was wrong.

I said he left me with no money
And he pulled out 400, cash,
Which I snatched out of his hand
        Never looking back to see if he cared.

All these years later I still don't know
If I was just too fast, or if he let me go…

And I'm not sure which version I prefer.

Listless and Learning

It's very simple:
I live in a fiction I'm no longer writing.

"Don't treat people like opportunities,"
          I blurted drunkenly,
            "Even if they want you to."

Because now I can sense where the truth is
But I dance around it,
Grasping and groping,

And I know you couldn't hear me but I meant what I said.

Don't treat people like opportunities,
Even if they want you to

—And I've always been a hands-on learner,

So that there's great wisdom in being mistreated,
          And it feels like the golden rule goes platinum.

The next day was like being beaten with sticks
Before getting out of bed,
            And you said:

"You used to believe in yourself but now you don't believe."

But I believe in a million things,
Just none that you can see, and none that I can point to.

I believe that no one should ever have to hurt so bad,
But that sometimes we do, in order to learn just that.

The Moth and the Flame

The unadorned bulb flickers off
Your radiant smile
Wine-faced pajama dreamer
          You hold
More beauty in your hopes than most
Fail to imagine. Winter is everywhere
In the soft glow of your frigid apartment
You curl your fragility under blankets
And nothing feels like cinematography
Strobe lights or canvas, no,
        This moment comes as is,
And I tremble at your breathing voice;
          You are
The encounter not bound in expression,
Where photographs fail and poets fall silent.
I hold your angled shoulders
In my thin and thawing hands
And imagine something eternal present
In the momentousness of our lives.

I suddenly understand,
How the moth is not confused by the flame;

As in silence,
        Your eyes produce my tears,
         Which I call joy.

Exaltation

The most talented people I know
All know each other.

               They meet
On weekday nights in quiet joints
You wouldn't otherwise notice, swallowed
By the city,
            Dusty trees in neon forests

Hip places because of hip people
               Also swallowed
Or so it seems to me
By the city coursing through them, they

Send it out
In poems songs and stories
               About vaguely
               Their love affairs and dreams

Heavy hearted angels

               They tuck their wings away
               When they go out in the world.

I met an angel at a rock club. She was standing just behind
me unassuming and it's not just that she was beautiful, she
was blinding and beaming, and like personality her smile
belied her confidence, and I guess confident enough to
display her girlish insecurity, like it was written in her eyes,
trapped in the moment of becoming, the brightest state of
being, and she smiled (how she smiled!), she seemed to
know the whole world except me and she—

she smiled as she shook my hand, I think because she knew
I was helpless. *Hello,* she said, *it's nice to finally meet you.*

Some of them, I think they know,
       Are too old to still be artists.
             It's a young person's game.

But we're about their age.

             —And I think that's why I say that
             I want to know their secret.

You know it; you just want to speak it.

The next time I met her we ducked into a corner as if in a
subsection of a subsection we began to feel we could say
anything and we talked for hours mostly about how some
people never get jaded they remain childlike in their
kindness generous and polite no matter how much they
know they don't let it get in the way of a dream and I told
her we should stop for a moment to take in the scene, and
not like a clique or a club but like a snapshot of life. I said
we were at an extraordinary place to know beautiful
brilliant people and to love them and what a shame that we
all have to go back out there alone. I said I had to go home,
to get some sleep before morning, and she said,
             Take me with you.

There's something in human nature
That will always want perfection
          And maybe it's because
          We know we belong with God

110

That uneasiness
That we're just not good enough

And that craziness
That we can actually get there with some effort.

We all have a vision of a life that no one has.

Why be miserable for what you lack
When you can be happy for what you have?

Maybe that's what they know.
Maybe that's their glow.
—What about you,
How do you stay like this?

I'm not always like this,
I get very dark.

I want to see that. I want to be with you for it.

Impossible.
You're what takes it away.

It seemed like we never left each other as we supported and
sustained each other and although we never spent much
time in the same place we were never apart and we always
felt at home. We talked for weeks about the vulnerability
and power of codependency as if we were standing in the
rain discussing the water, and I constantly asked her if she
knew how I loved her.

Love is most strange in the way it takes two,
How it won't support itself alone
                          But needs a spatial home
And how lovers
Are like subsections
          Of whatever reality doesn't matter to them.

                    I used to pray for someone like you.

                    I never dreamt of anything so great;
                    I pray for you now that you're here.

She was an artist like I never could have imagined and her
vast talent put me in perspective; she spent her mornings
rebuilding the ruins of my heart and at night she would sing
my dreams alive, and every day I'd spend with her was like
a comfortable surprise. She was both everything I wanted
and somehow something more, and every time I'd return
from the world outside I would find new paintings on my
windowless walls…   and I don't believe in one-sided doors.

The difference between people and God
Is that when you go towards God
He is already there.
                    He loves you before you know Him.

People though, they're always walking away.
If they don't go towards each other
          Then love just gets lost on the wind.

112

Heaven must be where no one is lost.
Where everybody already loves you.

I don't remember how long she was here and some days I
can't even remember what she looked like but I still think I
see her in places she couldn't be in places people can't
occupy and I cry, like a child I cry, when I think of her in the
back of dusky nowhere barrooms full of smiling geniuses
and it's like they love me because she forced them and I
know she's somewhere and that place is better but I worry,
all the time I worry, because I want to be sure that she's not
feeling too dark.

Life is almost arbitrary
Because we too get scattered on the wind
        In the vastness of existence,

But I say almost, because God understands
What we can't comprehend
    In the matters of meaning and love.

Sometimes people have to go
To where others can't follow
And what a terrible thing it is
                        For love

To watch as they walk away.

Take me with you! I was screaming at her, the closest I ever
came to being angry, but she smiled (God how she smiled!)
because she knew that I wasn't and she seemed to summon
a strength that she never had before, an expert at the

unavoidable like she was a million years old with the heart of a child, but I'll never forget that when she left I could hear her sobbing through the door, and I don't know how long it's been but it feels like forever and my heart feels heavy and ancient and just last night I was sitting in the back of a secret location when I overheard the sweet angelic whispers of two joyful artists smiling my way, saying "he's always writing to her, even though she's gone."

God is always with us
Helping with our tear-soaked hearts
        And we get lost and pray.
        We pray to get back home.

We hope Heaven is an eternal snapshot
Of the brightest state of being
Where we'll all be reunited
        And never say goodbye again.

So this is the end... What will you do?

I will try to remember to smile
And I will never forget you...
    I will try my best, because that is all we can do.
        What about you?

I will never leave.
I will stay right here
    Hidden away from the world
    In quiet places,

            And I'll surround myself
            By good and talented dreamers
                And I will try my best.

I will try to put myself
Into a work of art

So that you can take me with you.

                She is sobbing on the other side of the door
                And I whisper it again
                This time as if sending it out into the world
                    As if praying it into the wind:

                Take me with you.

Breinigsville, PA USA
29 March 2010
235099BV00001B/14/P